A QUICK HISTORY ON AI

THE RISE, IMPACT AND FUTURE OF ARTIFICIAL INTELLIGENCE

LIAM HENRY JR

Copyright © 2024 by Liam Henry Jr

All rights reserved. No part of this publication may be reproduced, distributed, or transmitted in any form or by any means, including photocopying, recording, or other electronic or mechanical methods, without the prior written permission of the publisher, except in the case of brief quotations embodied in critical reviews and certain other non commercial uses permitted by copyright law.

Table of Contents

Preface: A Glimpse into the Future, Rooted in the Past

Introduction: A Spark of Intelligence in Machines

Chapter 1: Early Days of Artificial Intelligence (Antiquity - 1950s)

1.1 Ancient Myths and Ideas: Seeds of Artificial Intelligence

1.2 The Rise of Logic and Mechanics: Building the Mechanical Mind

1.3 The Birth of Modern AI (1950s): The Dawn of the Digital Age

1.4 Conclusion: A Legacy of Ideas and Inventions

Chapter 2: Foundational Decades (1950s-1980s): A Period of Promise, Challenges, and Transformation

2.1 Early Optimism and Funding (1950s-1960s): A Golden Age of Promise

2.2 Early Achievements and Limitations (1960s-1970s): A Reality Check for AI

2.3 The Rise and Fall of Expert Systems (1960s-1980s): A Promising Approach with Growing Pains

2.4 The AI Winter (1970s-1980s): A Cooling Down After a Hype-Filled Summer

2.5 New Directions and Emerging Techniques (1970s-1980s): Seeds of a Future Explosion

2.6 Conclusion: A Period of Growth and Lessons Learned

Chapter 3: Renewed Focus and Advancements (1980s-Present): The Rise of Deep Learning and the AI Revolution

3.1 The Dawn of Deep Learning: Rekindling the Flame of Innovation

3.2 Deep Learning Revolutionizes AI: From Theory to Transformative Power

3.3 The Expanding Reach of AI: Deep Learning's Impact Across Industries

3.4 Ethical Considerations and Challenges: Navigating the Responsible Development of AI

3.5 Conclusion: A New Era of AI - A Look Back and a Look Forward

Chapter 4: Neural Networks

4.1 McCulloch & Pitts and the Groundwork for Neural Networks (1943)

4.2 Frank Rosenblatt and the Perceptron (1957)

Chapter 5 on Natural Language Processing (NLP)

5.1 ELIZA (1965): A Pioneering Chatbot

5.2 Impact of GPT-3 Release:

Chapter 6: Machine Learning

6.1 Newell and Simon's General Problem Solver (GPS) (1967)

Chapter 7: Robotics

7.1 iRobot introduces Roomba (2002)

Chapter 8: DeepMind

8.1 AlphaGo defeats world champion Lee Sedol (2015)

8.2 AlphaZero defeats the world's best chess and shogi engines (2017)

Chapter 9: The Impact of Artificial Intelligence

9.1 Expert Systems (1980s)

9.2 IBM's Deep Blue defeats chess world champion Kasparov (1997)

9.3 IBM's Watson defeats two former Jeopardy! champions (2011)

Chapter 10: The Future of Artificial Intelligence

10.1 OpenAI releases GPT-3 (2020)

10.2 Google's LaMDA (2023)

10.3 Legal issues around AI art creation (2023)

Conclusion

Preface: A Glimpse into the Future, Rooted in the Past

Artificial intelligence (AI) has become an inescapable force in our world, woven into the fabric of our daily lives. From the moment you wake up to a smart alarm on a voice-activated device to the personalized recommendations on your favorite streaming service, AI is silently shaping our experiences. Yet, for many, AI remains a mysterious and sometimes intimidating concept.

This book aims to bridge that gap. We will embark on a journey through the history of AI, tracing its evolution from the realm of philosophical thought and ancient myths to the sophisticated machines of today. We will explore the early optimism and setbacks, the groundbreaking advancements in deep learning, and the ever-expanding array of AI applications.

However, this book is not merely a historical account. By understanding the past, we can gain valuable insights into the future of AI. We will delve into the ethical considerations that accompany this powerful technology and explore the potential challenges and opportunities it presents.

This book is written for anyone curious about the world of AI, regardless of technical background. It is designed to be accessible and engaging, providing a comprehensive overview of this rapidly evolving field. Whether you are a student, a professional, or simply someone with a keen interest in the future, this book will equip you with the knowledge to understand, navigate, and even contribute to the remarkable world of artificial intelligence.

As we stand at the precipice of a future increasingly shaped by AI, it is crucial to have informed discussions and responsible development. This book invites you to join the conversation, to understand the history that brought us here, and to collectively shape the future of artificial intelligence.

Introduction: A Spark of Intelligence in Machines

The human mind has always been fascinated by the possibility of creating intelligent machines. From ancient myths of artificial beings to the sophisticated robots and computer programs of today, the quest for artificial intelligence (AI) has captured our imagination for centuries.

This book delves into the captivating history of AI, exploring its early roots, revolutionary advancements, and the profound impact it has on our world. We will trace the path from philosophical ideas to the machines that are transforming our lives.

This journey will explore:

The seeds of AI sown in ancient myths and philosophical inquiries.

The birth of modern AI research and the groundbreaking Turing Test.

The periods of optimism, setbacks, and renewed focus that shaped the field.

The rise of deep learning and its transformative power for AI applications.

The ethical considerations and potential challenges that come with intelligent machines.

As we embark on this exploration, we will not only understand the history of AI but also gain insights into its potential to shape our future. This book will equip you to:

Appreciate the remarkable achievements in AI research and development.

Understand the core concepts and techniques that drive AI applications.

Grasp the profound impact AI has on various aspects of our lives.

Engage in informed discussions about the future of AI and its potential benefits and challenges.

Get ready to embark on a fascinating journey into the world of artificial intelligence!

Chapter 1: Early Days of Artificial Intelligence (Antiquity - 1950s)

The dream of creating intelligent machines stretches back centuries, long before the invention of computers and the birth of modern AI research. This chapter explores the fascinating early days of AI, where the seeds of this revolutionary field were first sown.

1.1 Ancient Myths and Ideas: Seeds of Artificial Intelligence

Long before the whirring of computers and the hum of robots, the human imagination dreamt of intelligent machines. These early notions, born in the realm of myth and philosophy, planted the seeds for the field of artificial intelligence (AI).

Mythological Marvels:

Across various cultures, myths depict artificial beings with human-like capabilities. Here are a few prominent examples: * **Greek Mythology:** Hephaestus, the god of fire and metalworking, was renowned for crafting ingenious creations, including automatons - self-moving machines. These included robotic servants like Talos, a giant bronze automaton who guarded Crete. * **Jewish Folklore:** The Golem, a creature from Jewish mythology, was an animated being formed from clay and brought to life through mystical rituals. These stories explored the concept of imbuing life into inanimate objects.

Philosophical Ponderings:

While myths were fantastical, they sparked philosophical debates about the nature of intelligence and the possibility of machines replicating it. Early philosophers like: **Aristotle:** Contemplated the distinction between potential and actuality, questioning whether machines could ever possess the potential for thought and reason. **René Descartes:** Famous for his "cogito, ergo sum" (I think, therefore I am) proposition, grappled with the definition of what constitutes a mind and whether machines could ever possess one.

These early explorations, both mythical and philosophical, laid the groundwork for future inquiries into artificial intelligence. They fueled the human desire to understand and potentially create intelligent machines, paving the way for advancements in the centuries to come.

1.2 The Rise of Logic and Mechanics: Building the Mechanical Mind

The early days of AI weren't just about fantastical myths. The 17th and 18th centuries saw a confluence of two key developments that further fueled the dream of intelligent machines: the rise of mechanics and the development of formal logic.

The Mechanical Marvels:

The fascination with automata, intricate mechanical devices that could perform complex actions, grew significantly. These ingenious creations captured the public imagination and blurred the line between simple machines and potentially intelligent ones. Here are some prominent examples: **Vaucanson's Automaton Duck (1738):** This life-sized mechanical duck could flap its wings, quack, and even peck at grain. Its intricate design and realistic behavior fueled speculation about the possibilities of creating even more complex machines. **Jacques de Vaucanson's The Digesting Lion (1738):** This even more sophisticated automaton appeared to eat food and excrete waste products, further blurring the lines between mechanical and potentially "alive" constructs.

The Formidable Formulations of Logic:

Alongside the advancements in mechanics, philosophers like Gottfried Wilhelm Leibniz pursued a different avenue for creating intelligence: logic. Leibniz envisioned a "universal language of thought," a system that could represent all knowledge and reasoning processes using symbols and rules. **Leibniz's Calculus Ratiocinator:** This theoretical system aimed to solve problems and arguments through logical deduction, laying the foundation for symbolic AI, a dominant approach in early AI research that focused on representing knowledge and reasoning in symbolic structures like logic statements.

The rise of mechanics demonstrated the possibility of building complex machines that mimicked some aspects of living creatures. Meanwhile, advancements in formal logic provided a framework for representing and manipulating information, paving the way for developing algorithms for intelligent reasoning. These combined developments fueled the growing belief in the potential for creating machines with human-like intelligence.

1.3 The Birth of Modern AI (1950s): The Dawn of the Digital Age

The 1950s marked a turning point in the history of AI. The invention of programmable computers provided the physical platform needed to translate theoretical ideas about artificial intelligence into practical realities.

The Digital Revolution:

The development of electronic computers in the mid-20th century offered a powerful tool for implementing algorithms and theories related to AI. These machines, unlike their mechanical predecessors, could be programmed to perform complex calculations and manipulate information at high speeds. This opened doors for researchers to explore new avenues for creating intelligent machines.

Alan Turing and the Turing Test:

A pivotal moment in the birth of modern AI came in 1950 with the publication of Alan Turing's groundbreaking paper, "Computing Machinery and Intelligence." This paper introduced the now-famous Turing Test, a test of a machine's ability to exhibit intelligent behavior equivalent to, or indistinguishable from, that of a human. * The Turing Test involved a human interrogator conversing with two hidden entities, one being a human and the other a machine. If the interrogator could not reliably tell the difference based solely on the conversation, the machine was considered to have achieved human-level intelligence.

Turing's work not only provided a benchmark for evaluating AI progress but also sparked a vibrant debate about the nature of intelligence and the possibility of machines achieving it. This paper is widely considered to be the foundational work of modern AI research.

1.3.1 Early AI Programs:

The availability of computers spurred the development of early AI programs. Here are a few noteworthy examples:

```
* **Samuel's Checkers-Playing Program (1950s):**
This program, developed by Arthur Samuel, learned
and improved its checkers-playing ability through
```

```
machine learning techniques, demonstrating the
potential for machines to learn from experience.
*   **Newell and Simon's Logic Theorist (1956):**
This program aimed to solve logic problems using
symbolic reasoning, showcasing the potential of
AI for tasks traditionally considered to require
human intelligence.
```

The 1950s marked a significant shift in the field of AI. With the advent of computers and the groundbreaking work of Alan Turing, the dream of creating intelligent machines was no longer confined to myths and philosophy. The stage was set for a new era of exploration and development in the field of artificial intelligence.

1.4 Conclusion: A Legacy of Ideas and Inventions

The journey through the early days of AI has unveiled a fascinating interplay between imagination and innovation. From the fantastical creations in ancient myths to the birth of modern AI research, this chapter has explored the intellectual and technological foundations upon which this field has been built.

Looking Back, Moving Forward

The early days of AI established a rich legacy of ideas and inventions.

Ancient myths sparked curiosity about intelligent machines.

Philosophical inquiries explored the nature of intelligence.

The rise of mechanics demonstrated the potential for building complex machines.

Advancements in logic provided a framework for representing and manipulating information.

The invention of computers offered a powerful platform for implementing AI algorithms.

Alan Turing's Turing Test provided a benchmark for evaluating AI progress.

These early explorations laid the groundwork for the remarkable advancements in AI we see today.

The next chapter will delve into the foundational decades of AI (1950s-1980s), exploring periods of optimism, setbacks, and the emergence of new approaches that shaped the field. We will see how the seeds sown in the early days blossomed into a vibrant research area with real-world applications.

Chapter 2: Foundational Decades (1950s-1980s): A Period of Promise, Challenges, and Transformation

The 1950s to 1980s were foundational decades for artificial intelligence (AI) research. This period witnessed bursts of optimism fueled by early successes, followed by periods of setbacks due to the limitations of technology and the complexity of human intelligence. However, these decades also saw the emergence of new approaches and significant advancements that laid the groundwork for the AI revolution we see today.

2.1 Early Optimism and Funding (1950s-1960s): A Golden Age of Promise

The dawn of the 1950s marked a golden age of optimism for artificial intelligence (AI) research. The groundwork had been laid by Alan Turing's foundational work and the arrival of powerful computers. This period was fueled by a sense of immense potential and the belief that significant progress towards human-level AI was within reach.

A Fertile Ground for Innovation:

The birth of modern AI research in the 1950s created a fertile ground for innovation. Researchers were brimming with ideas and enthusiasm, fueled by the possibilities unlocked by computers.

Early successes like the problem-solving capabilities of Newell and Simon's Logic Theorist and the learning ability of Samuel's Checkers-Playing Program further bolstered this optimism. These programs, though limited, demonstrated the potential of AI for tasks traditionally thought to require human intelligence.

A Flood of Funding:

The early achievements of AI research captured the imagination not just of scientists but also of policymakers and the public. Governments and research institutions recognized the potential of AI and poured funding into the field.

This financial support allowed researchers to pursue ambitious projects and experiment with new ideas, accelerating the pace of progress in AI research.

A Catalyst for Collaboration:

The influx of funding also fostered collaboration between researchers from different disciplines like computer science, mathematics, psychology, and linguistics. This cross-pollination of ideas further enriched the field and led to the development of new approaches to AI.

However, this era of optimism was not without its limitations:

Overly Ambitious Timelines: Fueled by enthusiasm, some researchers made overly ambitious predictions about the timeline for achieving human-level AI. These predictions, when not met, would contribute to disillusionment in later years.

Limited Computing Power: The computers of the 1950s and 1960s, though powerful for their time, still lacked the processing capabilities needed for complex AI algorithms. This limited the scope and sophistication of what researchers could achieve.

Despite these limitations, the early optimism and funding of the 1950s and 1960s laid a crucial foundation for the field of AI. The groundwork established in this period would pave the way for the development of new techniques and the eventual explosion of AI in the latter decades of the 20th century and beyond.

2.2 Early Achievements and Limitations (1960s-1970s): A Reality Check for AI

The 1960s and 1970s were a period of both achievement and reckoning for artificial intelligence (AI) research. While early successes fueled excitement, researchers began to grapple with the limitations of existing approaches and the immense complexity of human intelligence.

Early Wins: Demonstrating Potential

Problem-Solving Power: Programs like Newell and Simon's General Problem Solver (GPS) showcased AI's ability to solve complex problems using logical reasoning and search techniques. This laid the groundwork for expert systems, a key development in this era.

Learning from Experience: Samuel's Checkers-Playing Program, which learned and improved its game through playing experience, demonstrated the potential for machine learning, a crucial concept in modern AI.

Natural Language Processing (NLP) Beginnings: Early attempts at NLP, like ELIZA, a program simulating a Rogerian therapist, emerged, showcasing the potential for AI to interact with humans using natural language.

The Inevitable Roadblocks

The Bottleneck of Computing Power: The computational limitations of the time hampered the development of more sophisticated AI algorithms. Processing power simply couldn't keep pace with the complexity researchers envisioned.

The Brittleness of Early Approaches: AI programs excelled at specific tasks within narrow domains but lacked the flexibility and adaptability of the human mind. They struggled to handle situations outside their programmed parameters.

The Knowledge Acquisition Bottleneck: Expert systems, designed to capture human expertise in specific domains, faced challenges in encoding vast amounts of knowledge into a usable format. The process was time-consuming, expensive, and limited the scalability of these systems.

A Shift in Focus: The Rise of Expert Systems

From General Intelligence to Targeted Solutions: Recognizing the limitations of achieving human-level intelligence in the near future, researchers shifted focus to developing expert systems.

Capturing Human Expertise: These systems aimed to replicate the knowledge and decision-making capabilities of human experts in specific areas like medicine, finance, or engineering.

Successes and Shortcomings: Expert systems achieved some notable successes, providing valuable decision-making support in various domains. However, their limitations in handling new situations and the knowledge acquisition bottleneck became apparent over time.

The era of the 1960s and 1970s for AI research was a time of both significant strides and a reality check. Early achievements demonstrated the potential of AI, but limitations in technology and the sheer complexity of human intelligence forced a shift in focus. The groundwork laid during this period, however, proved crucial for the development of more sophisticated techniques like deep learning that would revolutionize AI in the years to come.

2.3 The Rise and Fall of Expert Systems (1960s-1980s): A Promising Approach with Growing Pains

Expert systems emerged in the 1960s as a beacon of hope in the field of artificial intelligence (AI) research. These systems aimed to capture the knowledge and reasoning capabilities of human experts in specific domains, offering promising solutions for complex problems. However, their limitations and challenges ultimately led to their decline in the 1980s.

The Promise of Expertise in a Machine

Knowledge Codification: Expert systems offered a way to codify human expertise into a computer program. This promised to make valuable knowledge accessible and transferable, overcoming limitations of human memory and availability.

Decision-Making Support: These systems aimed to assist human experts in solving problems and making decisions by providing reasoning capabilities and access to a vast knowledge base.

Early Successes: Expert systems achieved some notable successes in various fields. For instance, XCON, an expert system from Digital Equipment Corporation (DEC), configured computer systems, reducing errors and saving the company millions of dollars.

The Cracks Begin to Show

Knowledge Acquisition Bottleneck: Encoding vast amounts of human expertise into a usable format proved to be a time-consuming and expensive process. Extracting and formalizing knowledge from human experts was a complex task.

Limited Reasoning Power: While expert systems excelled at reasoning within their specific domain, they struggled to handle novel situations or problems outside their predefined knowledge base. Their inflexibility limited their broader applicability.

Maintenance Challenges: Keeping expert systems up-to-date with the latest knowledge and evolving practices was a significant challenge. The dynamic nature of many fields rendered these systems outdated quickly.

The Fall from Grace: The AI Winter Descends

Disillusionment Sets In: The limitations of expert systems, coupled with the failure of AI research to achieve the ambitious goals set in earlier decades, led to a period of disillusionment known as the "AI Winter."

Funding Dries Up: As enthusiasm waned, government funding for AI research declined significantly, hindering further development in the field.

Lessons Learned: A Legacy for Future Advancements

Despite their shortcomings, expert systems played a crucial role in the history of AI. They demonstrated the potential of AI for practical applications and laid the groundwork for future knowledge-based systems.

The challenges faced by expert systems highlighted the importance of knowledge representation, reasoning under uncertainty, and the need for more adaptable and flexible AI systems.

The rise and fall of expert systems offer valuable lessons for the field of AI. It serves as a reminder of the importance of a balanced approach, focusing on both practical applications and fundamental research. The knowledge and experience gained during this era would contribute to the advancements in machine learning and deep learning that would propel AI research forward in the latter part of the 20th century.

2.4 The AI Winter (1970s-1980s): A Cooling Down After a Hype-Filled Summer

The 1970s and 1980s witnessed a period of decline in enthusiasm and funding for artificial intelligence (AI) research, known as the "AI Winter." This era followed a period of immense optimism and ambitious goals that were not met with the anticipated breakthroughs.

The Seeds of Disillusionment

Unrealistic Timelines: Early predictions about the rapid development of human-level AI proved overly optimistic. The complexity of human intelligence and the limitations of existing technology became apparent.

The Brittleness of Early Approaches: AI programs of the time struggled with tasks outside their specific training data. Their lack of flexibility and adaptability dampened enthusiasm for the field's potential.

The Limitations of Expert Systems: While initially promising, expert systems faced challenges in knowledge acquisition and maintenance. Their inability to handle complex or novel situations exposed their limitations.

A Harsh Reality Check

Funding Cuts: As the initial excitement waned, government funding for AI research declined significantly. This limited the resources available for researchers to pursue new ideas and overcome existing challenges.

Shifting Public Perception: The media, which had previously hyped the potential of AI, began to portray the field in a negative light, focusing on unfulfilled promises and setbacks. This shift in public perception further hampered enthusiasm and support.

A Period of Reassessment

Not a Complete Standstill: Despite the funding cuts, AI research did not completely grind to a halt. Researchers continued to explore alternative approaches and develop new techniques, laying the groundwork for future advancements.

The Rise of Connectionism: This period saw a renewed interest in connectionism, a form of artificial intelligence inspired by the structure and function of the human brain. This would pave the way for the development of artificial neural networks in later years.

Lessons Learned: The AI Winter served as a valuable learning experience. It highlighted the importance of setting realistic goals, focusing on fundamental research, and acknowledging the complexity of human intelligence.

The AI Winter, though a period of decline, proved to be a necessary pause for reflection and redirection. It forced researchers to reassess their approaches and ultimately led to the development of new techniques that would fuel the explosion of AI in the decades to come.

2.5 New Directions and Emerging Techniques (1970s-1980s): Seeds of a Future Explosion

The "AI Winter" of the 1970s and 1980s, though a period of decline in funding and enthusiasm, wasn't devoid of progress. This era witnessed the exploration of alternative approaches and the development of new techniques that would lay the groundwork for the future explosion of artificial intelligence (AI).

A Shift in Focus: Beyond Symbolic AI

The Limitations of Logic-Based Systems: Symbolic AI, the dominant approach in early AI research, relied on manipulating symbols and rules to represent knowledge and reasoning. However, this approach struggled to capture the complexity of real-world problems.

The Rise of Connectionism: Researchers began to explore connectionism, also known as artificial neural networks (ANNs). Inspired by the structure and function of the human brain, ANNs consist of interconnected nodes that process information in a distributed manner.

Paving the Way for Deep Learning

Challenges with Early ANNs: While conceptually promising, early ANNs faced limitations in training and processing power. The lack of powerful computing resources and efficient training algorithms hindered their development.

Marvin Minsky and Seymour Papert's Perceptrons: This influential book (1969) highlighted limitations of early ANNs, leading to a temporary decline in their research. However, it also sparked discussions about overcoming these limitations and paved the way for future advancements.

Alternative Approaches Emerge

Probabilistic Reasoning: This approach focused on representing and reasoning with uncertainty, which is inherent in many real-world problems. This would prove valuable for tasks like machine learning and robotics.

Evolutionary Computation: Inspired by natural selection, these algorithms mimicked the process of evolution to optimize solutions for complex problems.

A Period of Quiet Progress

Despite the funding cuts, dedicated researchers continued to explore new ideas and refine existing techniques. This period laid the groundwork for the breakthroughs in deep learning and other areas that would revolutionize AI in the late 20th and early 21st centuries.

The Legacy of the AI Winter

The AI Winter served as a crucial turning point. It forced researchers to re-evaluate their approaches and acknowledge the complexity of human intelligence.

The seeds sown during this period, particularly the development of connectionism and alternative reasoning techniques, would blossom into powerful tools that would propel AI research forward in the coming decades.

2.6 Conclusion: A Period of Growth and Lessons Learned

The foundational decades of AI research (1950s-1980s) were a period of both remarkable growth and significant challenges. This era witnessed the birth of modern AI research, fueled by early optimism and groundbreaking ideas. However, it also exposed the limitations of existing approaches and the immense complexity of human intelligence.

Key Takeaways from the Foundational Decades:

Early Optimism and Achievements: The 1950s and 1960s were marked by a surge of enthusiasm for AI research. Early successes with programs like Newell and Simon's Logic Theorist and Samuel's Checkers-Playing Program demonstrated the potential of AI for problem-solving and learning.

The Rise and Fall of Expert Systems: The 1960s and 1970s saw the development and subsequent decline of expert systems. While these systems offered a way to capture human expertise in specific domains, they faced limitations in knowledge acquisition and inflexibility in adapting to new situations.

The AI Winter: A Period of Reassessment: The funding cuts and disillusionment of the 1970s and 1980s, though challenging, proved to be a valuable learning experience. It forced researchers to re-evaluate their approaches and focus on more realistic goals.

New Directions and Emerging Techniques: Despite the funding slowdown, the foundational decades saw the exploration of alternative approaches like connectionism, which laid the groundwork for the rise of deep learning in later years.

A Foundation for the Future

The lessons learned from the foundational decades would propel AI research forward. The groundwork established in this period, including the development of new techniques and a more realistic understanding of the challenges involved, would pave the way for the remarkable advancements in deep learning and other areas of AI that define the field today. The next chapter will delve into the revolution brought about by deep learning and explore the transformative impact of AI on various aspects of our world.

Chapter 3: Renewed Focus and Advancements (1980s-Present): The Rise of Deep Learning and the AI Revolution

The embers of innovation from the foundational decades of AI research (1950s-1980s) rekindled into a blazing fire in the late 20th and early 21st centuries. This chapter explores the revolution brought about by deep learning, a powerful technique that has transformed the field of artificial intelligence and its impact on various aspects of our world.

3.1 The Dawn of Deep Learning: Rekindling the Flame of Innovation

The late 20th and early 21st centuries witnessed a resurgence of interest in artificial intelligence (AI), fueled by a powerful new technique: deep learning. This section delves into the key factors that paved the way for this revolution.

Building on the Legacy of Connectionism

Deep learning isn't entirely new. It builds upon the concept of artificial neural networks (ANNs) introduced in the earlier decades of AI research. These ANNs are loosely inspired by the structure and function of the human brain. They consist of interconnected nodes, or artificial neurons, that process information and learn from patterns.

Overcoming Bottlenecks of Early ANNs

While conceptually promising, early ANNs faced limitations that hindered their development:

* **Computational Power:** Training complex ANNs with many layers of interconnected nodes required immense processing power. Early computers simply weren't powerful enough to handle the demands of deep learning algorithms.
* **Training Challenges:** Efficient training algorithms were needed to enable these complex networks to learn effectively from vast amounts of data.

The Rise of Powerful Hardware

The dawn of deep learning coincided with a significant advancement in hardware:

* **Graphics Processing Units (GPUs):** Originally designed for accelerating graphics processing in computers, GPUs turned out to be remarkably well-suited for the parallel processing requirements of deep learning algorithms. Their ability to handle massive amounts of data computations at high speeds proved to be a game-changer.

The Key Ingredient: Efficient Training Algorithms

The development of efficient training algorithms addressed another crucial bottleneck:

* **Backpropagation:** This algorithm revolutionized the way neural networks learn. It allowed the network to adjust the weights of its connections based on the errors made in its predictions. This iterative process enabled deep

learning models to learn complex patterns from vast datasets.

The Perfect Storm: A New Era Begins

The convergence of these factors - the theoretical foundation of connectionism, the availability of powerful GPUs, and the development of efficient training algorithms like backpropagation - created the perfect storm for the rise of deep learning. This powerful new technique would revolutionize various aspects of AI research and applications.

3.2 Deep Learning Revolutionizes AI: From Theory to Transformative Power

The dawn of deep learning wasn't just a technological advancement; it was a paradigm shift in AI. This section explores how deep learning has transformed various subfields of AI, leading to breakthroughs that were once unimaginable.

Image Recognition: Seeing the World Through Machines

Convolutional Neural Networks (CNNs): A specific type of deep learning architecture, CNNs are particularly adept at image recognition tasks. They excel at identifying patterns and extracting features from visual data.

From Blurry Vision to Human-Level Accuracy: Deep learning has revolutionized image recognition. CNNs can now achieve near-human-level accuracy in tasks like facial recognition, object detection in images and videos, and image classification. These advancements have applications in various fields, from [self-driving cars](URL self driving cars ON Wikipedia en.wikipedia.org) to [medical image analysis](URL medical image analysis in ai ON National Institutes of Health (.gov) nih.gov).

Natural Language Processing (NLP): Understanding and Generating Human Language

Deep Learning's Impact on NLP: Deep learning has significantly transformed NLP, enabling machines to understand and process human language with unprecedented sophistication.

From Chatbots to Machine Translation: Deep learning algorithms are now powering chatbots that can hold natural conversations, machine translation systems that can translate languages with impressive fluency, and sentiment analysis tools that can gauge the emotions and opinions expressed in text.

Speech Recognition: Bridging the Gap Between Speech and Machines

Beyond Text: Deep learning isn't limited to understanding written language. It has also significantly improved speech recognition accuracy.

From Dictation Software to Voice Assistants: Deep learning algorithms are behind the impressive speech recognition capabilities of virtual assistants like Siri and Alexa. They also power automatic speech recognition software used for tasks like voice-to-text transcription.

These are just a few examples of how deep learning has revolutionized core areas of AI research. By enabling machines to learn complex patterns from vast amounts of data, deep learning has opened doors to a new era of AI capabilities. The impact extends far beyond these core areas, influencing various fields like robotics, healthcare, and finance, as we will explore in the next section.

3.3 The Expanding Reach of AI: Deep Learning's Impact Across Industries

Deep learning's influence extends far beyond core AI subfields like image recognition, NLP, and speech recognition. It is transforming various industries, driving innovation and reshaping how we interact with technology in our everyday lives. Let's explore some of these exciting frontiers:

AI-Powered Robotics

From Repetitive Tasks to Complex Manipulation: Deep learning is propelling advancements in robotics. Robots are becoming more adept at performing tasks that were previously thought to require human dexterity and intelligence.

Deep Learning for Robotics: Deep learning algorithms enable robots to:

Perceive their environment: Through image and sensor data, robots can gain a better understanding of their surroundings and navigate complex spaces.

Learn from experience: Deep learning allows robots to continuously improve their performance by learning from past interactions and mistakes.

Adapt to new situations: Deep learning models can help robots adapt to novel situations and unforeseen circumstances.

Revolutionizing Healthcare

Deep Learning in Medical Applications: Deep learning is making waves in the healthcare sector by aiding in:

Medical image analysis: Deep learning algorithms can analyze medical scans like X-rays, MRIs, and CT scans with high accuracy, assisting doctors in early disease detection and diagnosis.

Drug discovery: By analyzing vast datasets of molecular structures and biological information, deep learning can accelerate drug discovery and development processes.

Personalized medicine: Deep learning can help tailor medical treatment plans to individual patients based on their unique medical history and genetic data.

Shaping the Financial Landscape

AI and Finance: Deep learning is impacting the financial sector in various ways, including:

Fraud detection: Deep learning models can analyze financial transactions to identify patterns indicative of fraudulent activity.

Algorithmic trading: Deep learning algorithms can be used to analyze market trends and make investment decisions at high speeds.

Risk assessment: Deep learning can help financial institutions assess the creditworthiness of borrowers and manage financial risks more effectively.

Beyond these examples, deep learning is making significant inroads in other fields such as:

Manufacturing: Deep learning can optimize production processes, improve quality control, and predict equipment failures.

Scientific Discovery: Deep learning can analyze complex scientific data to accelerate research breakthroughs and scientific discovery.

Entertainment: Deep learning is being used to create more realistic and immersive experiences in video games and virtual reality applications.

As deep learning continues to evolve and become more sophisticated, its impact on our world will continue to grow. However, alongside these advancements, it is crucial to address the ethical considerations and challenges associated with AI, as we will explore in the next section.

3.4 Ethical Considerations and Challenges: Navigating the Responsible Development of AI

The remarkable progress of deep learning has brought immense potential for good. However, alongside this progress lie significant ethical considerations and challenges that require careful attention to ensure the responsible development and deployment of AI. Here, we will delve into some of these key concerns:

Bias and Fairness:

Deep learning models are susceptible to inheriting biases present in the data they are trained on. This can lead to discriminatory outcomes, such as biased loan approvals or unfair hiring practices.

Mitigating Bias: Researchers and developers are actively working on techniques to mitigate bias in AI systems. This includes using diverse datasets, developing fairness metrics, and employing algorithmic debiasing techniques.

Explainability and Transparency:

Deep learning models, especially complex ones, can be opaque. Understanding how they arrive at their decisions can be challenging, raising concerns about accountability and trust.

Explainable AI (XAI): A growing field of research focuses on developing methods to make AI models more interpretable. This can help users understand the reasoning behind an AI's decision and identify potential biases.

The Future of Work:

Automation powered by AI has the potential to displace jobs in certain sectors. While new jobs will likely be created, there is a concern about the impact on workers whose skills become obsolete.

Reskilling and Upskilling: It is crucial to prepare the workforce for the changing job landscape. Governments, educational institutions, and businesses need to work together to provide opportunities for reskilling and upskilling workers to adapt to the demands of the AI-powered future.

Other Challenges:

Privacy Concerns: The increasing use of AI raises concerns about data privacy and security. As AI systems collect and analyze vast amounts of personal data, it is essential to ensure robust data protection measures are in place.

The Potential for Misuse: In the wrong hands, AI technology could be misused for malicious purposes. Safeguards and regulations are needed to prevent the misuse of AI for surveillance, weaponization, or other harmful applications.

The Road Ahead: Responsible AI Development

Addressing these ethical considerations is crucial for ensuring the responsible development and deployment of AI. Collaboration between researchers, developers, policymakers, and the public is essential to navigate these challenges and ensure that AI benefits all of humanity.

This section has only provided a brief overview of the ethical considerations surrounding AI. Further exploration of specific examples and ongoing debates in this field would be valuable additions to enrich this chapter.

3.5 Conclusion: A New Era of AI - A Look Back and a Look Forward

The rise of deep learning has ushered in a new era of artificial intelligence. No longer confined to research labs, AI is transforming industries, reshaping our daily lives, and influencing the future in profound ways. This chapter has explored this remarkable journey, from the early dreams of AI research to the powerful reality of deep learning.

A Recap: From Theory to Transformation

We began by examining the dawn of deep learning, where advancements in hardware and algorithms converged to create a powerful new technique. We then witnessed how deep learning revolutionized core AI subfields like image recognition, NLP, and speech recognition. Following that, we explored the expanding reach of AI, highlighting its impact on various industries like robotics, healthcare, and finance.

Challenges and Considerations: Navigating the Future

The journey isn't without its challenges. We discussed the ethical considerations surrounding AI, emphasizing the importance of mitigating bias, ensuring explainability and transparency, and preparing for the evolving world of work. These challenges necessitate responsible development and deployment of AI to ensure it benefits all of humanity.

Looking Ahead: A Collaborative Future

As we stand at the precipice of an AI-driven future, collaboration is key. Researchers, developers, policymakers, and the public must work together to address the challenges, establish ethical frameworks, and harness the immense potential of AI for positive change.

A Glimpse into the Future of AI

The field of AI is constantly evolving. Here are some exciting areas to consider exploring further:

The Rise of Explainable AI (XAI): As XAI techniques mature, AI systems will become more interpretable, fostering trust and enabling responsible deployment.

The Integration of AI and Robotics: The convergence of AI and robotics has the potential to create intelligent machines capable of complex tasks and real-world interaction.

The Democratization of AI: With advancements in cloud computing and open-source tools, AI development will become more accessible, leading to a broader range of applications and innovations.

The future of AI holds immense possibilities. By embracing the potential of this technology while addressing the challenges responsibly, we can work towards a future where AI serves as a powerful tool for progress and human flourishing.

Chapter 4: Neural Networks

Neural Networks *A Powerful Tool for Artificial Intelligence*

Speaker Notes In this chapter, we will embark on a fascinating exploration of neural networks. Neural networks are a powerful form of artificial intelligence (AI) inspired by the structure and function of the human brain. We will delve into their inner workings, understand how they learn and adapt, and explore the vast array of applications that neural networks have in today's world.

What are Neural Networks?

Biological Inspiration: Neural networks are inspired by the structure and function of the human brain.

Artificial Neurons: They consist of interconnected nodes called artificial neurons, which process information and learn from patterns.

Layered Architecture: Just like the human brain has billions of neurons connected by trillions of synapses, neural networks can have multiple layers of interconnected nodes. These layers include:

Input Layer: Receives the initial data.

Hidden Layers: Process and transform the data. (There can be multiple hidden layers)

Output Layer: Produces the final output of the network.

Speaker Notes Unlike traditional computer programs that follow a set of predetermined instructions, neural networks are fundamentally different. They have the remarkable ability to learn from data and improve their performance over time. This ability to learn and adapt makes them highly versatile and powerful tools for a wide range of applications.

How Neural Networks Work

Information Processing: Neural networks process information through layers of interconnected nodes.

Input Layer: Information enters the network through the input layer, where it is received and processed by the neurons.

Weighted Sums and Activation Functions: Each neuron applies a mathematical function (activation function) to a weighted sum of its inputs. These weights determine the influence of each input on the neuron's output.

Propagation: The output of a neuron is then passed on to the next layer of neurons, where it is further processed.

Final Output: This process continues until the final output layer is reached, which produces the network's final output.

Speaker Notes The connections between neurons are associated with weights. These weights signify the strength of the signal between neurons. During the all-important learning process, the weights are adjusted based on the network's performance. By fine-tuning these weights, the network can learn to recognize patterns in the data and progressively improve its accuracy over time.

Types of Neural Networks

A Diverse Toolbox: There are many different types of neural networks, each with its own strengths and applications.

Convolutional Neural Networks (CNNs): Particularly adept at image recognition and classification tasks, CNNs excel at identifying patterns in visual data.

Recurrent Neural Networks (RNNs): Well-suited for processing sequential data like text or speech, RNNs can handle tasks that involve order and relationships within the data.

Generative Adversarial Networks (GANs): Pioneering a new frontier, GANs can create entirely new and realistic data that closely resembles existing data.

Transformers: Particularly effective for natural language processing tasks, transformers are revolutionizing areas like machine translation and text summarization.

Speaker Notes The type of neural network chosen for a specific task depends on the nature of the data and the desired outcome. With ongoing research and development, new and innovative neural network architectures are constantly emerging, further expanding the capabilities of AI.

Learning in Neural Networks

4.1 McCulloch & Pitts and the Groundwork for Neural Networks (1943)

Speaker Notes In 1943, Warren McCulloch, a neurophysiologist, and Walter Pitts, a logician, published a groundbreaking paper titled "A Logical Calculus of the Ideas Immanent in Nervous Activity." This work laid the foundation for the development of artificial neural networks.

Key Contributions:

Mathematical Model of Neurons: McCulloch and Pitts introduced a simplified mathematical model of a neuron, now known as the McCulloch-Pitts neuron. This model represented a neuron as a binary classifier, meaning it could only output one of two values (often 0 or 1). It applied a weighted sum of its inputs to a threshold function to determine its output.

Building Blocks for Neural Networks: This model provided a fundamental building block for constructing neural networks. By connecting multiple McCulloch-Pitts neurons in layers, they showed the potential to create networks capable of complex computations.

Theoretical Framework: Their work established a theoretical framework for understanding how neural networks could process information and learn. This laid the groundwork for future research in artificial intelligence and neural networks.

Limitations:

Oversimplification: The McCulloch-Pitts neuron was a significant simplification of biological neurons. Real neurons are far more complex and exhibit non-binary outputs.

Limited Capabilities: The early neural networks inspired by this model had limited capabilities compared to modern networks.

Legacy:

Despite the limitations, the work of McCulloch and Pitts remains a landmark achievement. It sparked a new era of research in artificial intelligence and laid the groundwork for the development of the powerful neural networks we see today.

Speaker Notes The McCulloch-Pitts model, though simplistic, opened doors for significant advancements in the field of neural networks. It served as a springboard for further exploration and refinement, paving the way for the development of more complex and powerful neural network architectures that are transforming various industries today.

4.2 Frank Rosenblatt and the Perceptron (1957)

Speaker Notes Frank Rosenblatt, a prominent figure in the history of artificial intelligence, made a significant contribution in 1957 with the introduction of the Perceptron. The Perceptron can be viewed as a building block on the path to the development of modern neural networks.

Frank Rosenblatt was a prominent figure in the history of artificial intelligence.

In 1957, he introduced the Perceptron, a significant contribution to the field.

The Perceptron can be seen as a stepping stone towards the development of modern neural networks.

4.2.1

The Perceptron: A Single Layer Neural Network

Speaker Notes The Perceptron, introduced by Rosenblatt, is a single-layer neural network inspired by the McCulloch-Pitts neuron. It consists of an input layer, a single hidden layer with one neuron (also called the perceptron unit), and an output layer. Like the McCulloch-Pitts neuron, the perceptron unit applies a weighted sum of its inputs to an activation function (usually a threshold function) to produce a binary output (0 or 1).

The Perceptron, introduced by Rosenblatt, is a single-layer neural network.

It draws inspiration from the McCulloch-Pitts neuron.

The Perceptron is comprised of three layers: an input layer, a single hidden layer with one neuron (also known as the perceptron unit), and an output layer.

Similar to the McCulloch-Pitts neuron, the perceptron unit employs an activation function (often a threshold function) to a weighted sum of its inputs, ultimately generating a binary output (0 or 1).

4.2.2

Learning in the Perceptron

Speaker Notes The Perceptron utilizes a learning algorithm known as the perceptron learning rule. During training, the network is presented with input data and its desired output. The perceptron calculates its actual output based on the weighted sum of its inputs and the activation function. The difference between the desired output and the actual output is calculated as the error. The perceptron learning rule then adjusts the weights of the connections to reduce this error. This process is repeated iteratively until the network converges or reaches a minimum error level.

The Perceptron leverages a learning algorithm called the perceptron learning rule.

During training, the network encounters input data along with its corresponding desired output.

The perceptron calculates its actual output based on the activation function applied to a weighted sum of its inputs.

The discrepancy between the desired output and the actual output is computed as the error.

The perceptron learning rule then modifies the weights of the connections to minimize this error.

This process iterates until the network converges or achieves a minimum error level.

4.2.3

Limitations of the Perceptron

Speaker Notes Perceptrons have limitations in their capabilities. A single-layer perceptron can only learn linear relationships between the input data and the output. This limitation is known as the Perceptron limitation theorem, which states that a single-layer perceptron cannot classify datasets that are not linearly separable. (Imagine trying to separate data points consisting of overlapping circles with a straight line. A single perceptron cannot achieve this.)

Perceptrons are not without limitations in their capabilities.

Single-layer perceptrons are restricted to learning linear relationships between the input data and the output.

This limitation is referred to as the Perceptron limitation theorem. The theorem states that a single-layer perceptron is incapable of classifying datasets that are not linearly separable. (For instance, imagine attempting to separate data points representing overlapping circles using a straight line. A single perceptron cannot accomplish this task.)

4.2.4

Legacy of the Perceptron

Speaker Notes Rosenblatt's Perceptron, although limited in its capabilities, laid the groundwork for the development of more complex neural network architectures. The concept of a learning algorithm and the idea of training neural networks to perform specific tasks paved the way for future advancements. The resurgence of research in neural networks in the late 20th century and the development of powerful multi-layer neural networks owe a debt to the pioneering work of Rosenblatt and the Perceptron.

Despite its limitations, Rosenblatt's Perceptron paved the way for the development of more intricate neural network architectures.

The Perceptron introduced the concept of a learning algorithm and the notion of training neural networks to perform specific tasks. These ideas laid the foundation for future advancements in the field.

The resurgence of research in neural networks during the late 20th century and the creation of powerful multi-layer neural

Chapter 5 on Natural Language Processing (NLP)

Learning Analytics: Natural Language Processing as a Tool for Learning Analytics" by Laura K. Allen et al. discusses how NLP is used to analyze student written work and improve educational technology PDF.

5.1 ELIZA (1965): A Pioneering Chatbot

ELIZA, developed by Joseph Weizenbaum at MIT between 1964 and 1967, wasn't truly intelligent but became surprisingly influential in the field of Natural Language Processing (NLP). Here's a detailed breakdown:

What it Did:

ELIZA simulated conversation through a technique called pattern matching and keyword recognition.

Users typed sentences, and ELIZA searched for keywords or patterns within them.

Based on these patterns, ELIZA would respond with pre-programmed phrases or questions that often rephrased or reflected back the user's own words.

For example, if a user said, "I feel sad," ELIZA might respond with, "Tell me more about your sadness."

What it Wasn't:

ELIZA did not understand the meaning of the conversation. It simply manipulated keywords and sentence structures.

It couldn't hold a complex or factual conversation.

It had no real knowledge of the world.

Why it was Important:

Despite its limitations, ELIZA surprised people with its ability to simulate conversation and elicit emotional responses.

Users sometimes disclosed personal information to ELIZA, believing it understood them on a deeper level (known as the Eliza Effect).

This highlighted the power of human perception and our tendency to project human qualities onto machines.

ELIZA became a landmark program in the field of NLP, demonstrating the potential for human-computer interaction through language.

It sparked discussions about the nature of intelligence, communication, and the Turing Test, a test of a machine's ability to exhibit intelligent behavior equivalent to, or indistinguishable from, that of a human.

Further Exploration:

The original 1966 paper by Joseph Weizenbaum, "ELIZA—A Computer Program For The Study Of Natural Language Communication Between Man And Machine," provides a technical look at ELIZA's design [link to Stanford paper mentioned previously).

You can find a transcript of a conversation with ELIZA to get a feel for its interaction style [link to The Digital Antiquarian blog post mentioned previously).

ELIZA, though not truly intelligent, laid the groundwork for more sophisticated chatbots and NLP applications. It serves as a reminder of the importance of user perception and the challenges of achieving true human-like conversation with machines.

5.2 Impact of GPT-3 Release:

Scale: GPT-3 boasted 175 billion parameters, significantly larger than previous LLMs. This vastness allowed it to process information and generate human-quality text with more nuance and complexity.

Capabilities: GPT-3 could perform various tasks beyond simple text generation. It could translate languages, write different kinds of creative content, and answer questions in an informative way.

Accessibility: OpenAI initially provided limited access to GPT-3 through an API, sparking interest and research in the potential applications of LLMs.

Later Developments:

OpenAI API Updates: Since its release, OpenAI has continuously improved and updated GPT-3 through its API. This includes introducing new versions like GPT-3.5 with access to browse online information and fine-tuned models for specific tasks (e.g., ChatGPT).

Focus on Safety and Responsible Use: OpenAI has also emphasized the importance of responsible use of GPT-3, considering its potential for generating misleading or biased content.

Further Exploration:

OpenAI Blog: The OpenAI blog is a great resource to learn more about GPT-3, its applications, and ongoing developments https://openai.com/news/.

Wikipedia: The Wikipedia page on GPT-3 provides a comprehensive overview of the model's architecture, capabilities, and impact https://en.wikipedia.org/wiki/GPT-3.

Overall, the release of GPT-3 in 2020 marked a significant leap forward in LLM technology. It continues to evolve and influence the field of NLP, with ongoing discussions about its potential benefits and challenges.

Chapter 6: Machine Learning

1. **Introduction to Machine Learning:**

Definition of Machine Learning (ML) and its place within Artificial Intelligence (AI)

Different types of Machine Learning: Supervised learning, Unsupervised learning, Reinforcement learning

Applications of Machine Learning in various fields (e.g., healthcare, finance, recommendation systems)

2. **The Machine Learning Process:**

Data Collection and Preprocessing: Importance of data quality and preparing data for training algorithms.

Model Selection: Choosing the right ML algorithm for the specific task.

Training the Model: Feeding data into the algorithm and adjusting its parameters to improve performance.

Evaluation: Assessing the model's performance on unseen data and identifying potential biases.

3. **Common Machine Learning Algorithms:**

Linear regression: Predicting continuous values based on linear relationships.

Decision trees: Making predictions based on a series of yes/no questions.

Support Vector Machines (SVMs): Classifying data points into categories by creating a hyperplane.

K-Nearest Neighbors (KNN): Predicting based on the similarity of unseen data to known data points.

Neural Networks: Inspired by the structure of the brain, these models can learn complex patterns from data. (This might be a separate chapter in some resources)

4. Additional Topics (depending on the chapter's depth):

Overfitting and Underfitting: Balancing model complexity to avoid memorizing training data or generalizing poorly.

Feature Engineering: Creating new features from existing data to improve model performance.

Model Explainability: Understanding how a model makes decisions, especially for critical applications.

Ethical Considerations in Machine Learning: Addressing bias, fairness, and potential misuse of ML models.

6.1 Newell and Simon's General Problem Solver (GPS) (1967)

Newell and Simon's General Problem Solver (GPS), developed in 1967, was a pioneering program that aimed to be a universal problem-solving tool. Here's a deeper look at its contributions:

What it Was:

A Problem-Solving Framework: GPS wasn't a program designed for a specific task but rather a framework for solving any problem that could be represented in a particular way.

Means-Ends Analysis: It employed a "means-ends analysis" approach. This meant breaking down the difference between the current state and the desired goal state into smaller, achievable steps.

Problem Space: GPS operated within a "problem space" defined by:

Initial State: The starting point of the problem.

Operators: Actions that could transform the current state towards the goal.

Goal State: The desired outcome of the problem.

How it Worked:

Representing the Problem: The user had to encode the problem into the GPS framework, specifying the initial state, operators, and goal state.

Search: GPS used a search process to explore the problem space. It evaluated the difference between the current state and the goal state and applied operators that could reduce that difference.

Heuristics: To guide the search and avoid exploring every single possibility, GPS sometimes used heuristics, or "rules of thumb," to prioritize promising paths.

Impact and Limitations:

Innovation: GPS was a significant innovation as it separated the problem-solving knowledge (operators and goal states) from the general problem-solving strategy. This influenced future AI research.

Limitations: GPS had limitations. It struggled with problems that had a vast search space or required complex reasoning beyond simple means-ends analysis.

Real-World Challenges: GPS couldn't represent open-ended problems or problems with incomplete information, making real-world application difficult.

Further Exploration:

A Guide to the General Problem Solver Program GPS-2-2: This paper by Ernst and Newell delves deeper into the specific elements and workings of GPS [link unavailable due to source policy].

General Problem Solver (Wikipedia): The Wikipedia page on GPS provides a concise overview and additional references [https://en.wikipedia.org/wiki/General_Problem_Solver].

Overall, Newell and Simon's GPS laid the groundwork for symbolic AI and problem-solving research, demonstrating the potential for computers to tackle problems in a systematic manner. While its limitations became evident, GPS remains a crucial milestone in the development of Artificial Intelligence.

Chapter 7: Robotics

A Chapter 7 on Robotics would likely delve into the exciting world of machines that can sense, manipulate, and interact with the surrounding environment. Here's a breakdown of potential topics you might encounter:

1. Introduction to Robotics:

Definition of Robotics and its history

Different types of robots: Industrial robots, Service robots, Collaborative robots (cobots), Mobile robots, Aerial robots (drones)

Applications of robots in various fields (e.g., manufacturing, healthcare, exploration, logistics)

2. Components of a Robot:

Mechanics: The physical structure of a robot, including joints, linkages, and actuators (e.g., motors) that enable movement.

Sensors: Devices that allow robots to perceive their environment, such as cameras, LiDAR (Light Detection and Ranging), and touch sensors.

Control Systems: The "brain" of the robot, processing sensor data and sending commands to actuators for movement and action.

Power Source: Batteries, electrical grids, or internal combustion engines that provide energy for the robot.

3. Robotics Fundamentals:

Kinematics: The study of robot motion without considering the forces involved. This section might cover topics like robot arm geometry, degrees of freedom, and forward/inverse kinematics (calculating joint positions for desired end-effector positions).

Dynamics: The study of how forces and torques affect robot motion. This could involve concepts like inertia, torque control, and robot path planning (efficiently navigating the environment).

Perception: How robots interpret sensory data to understand their surroundings. This section might explore topics like computer vision, object recognition, and sensor fusion (combining data from multiple sensors).

4. Advanced Robotics Topics (depending on the chapter's depth):

Human-Robot Interaction (HRI): Principles for safe and effective collaboration between humans and robots.

Biomimicry in Robotics: Designing robots inspired by nature (e.g., snake robots for search and rescue).

Swarm Robotics: Coordination of multiple robots working together to achieve a common goal.

Artificial Intelligence (AI) in Robotics: Integrating AI algorithms for decision-making, learning, and adaptation in robots.

5. The Future of Robotics:

Ethical considerations in robotics (e.g., job displacement, safety concerns)

The potential impact of robots on society and the workforce

Emerging trends in robotics research (e.g., soft robotics, nano-robots)

By exploring these topics, Chapter 7 would equip you with a solid understanding of the fascinating field of robotics and its potential to shape the future.

7.1 iRobot introduces Roomba (2002)

A Pioneering Robotic Vacuum Cleaner:

First of its Kind: The Roomba was the first commercially available robotic vacuum cleaner for home use in the United States. It revolutionized the way people cleaned their floors, offering an automated solution for dirt and debris.

Automatic Cleaning: This disc-shaped robot featured sensors to navigate around furniture and obstacles, autonomously cleaning floors with a combination of brushes and suction.

Early Innovation: While not as sophisticated as today's Roombas, this first model paved the way for advancements in robot navigation, mapping, and cleaning capabilities.

Impact and Legacy:

Convenience and Time-Saving: Roomba offered a convenient way to maintain clean floors without manual effort, freeing up people's time for other activities.

Growth of Robot Vacuums: The Roomba's success spurred significant growth in the robot vacuum cleaner market, leading to a wider range of models and features from various manufacturers.

Evolving Technology: iRobot continues to develop and improve Roomba models, incorporating features like self-emptying bases, app control, and improved navigation for a more seamless cleaning experience.

Further Exploration:

iRobot Website: The iRobot website has a history section detailing the introduction of the Roomba https://about.irobot.com/history.

Robot Vacuum Cleaner Wikipedia Page: The Wikipedia page on robot vacuum cleaners provides a broader context for the Roomba's emergence https://en.wikipedia.org/wiki/Robotic_vacuum_cleaner.

The iRobot Roomba of 2002 stands as a testament to early robotic innovation in the home appliance market. It continues to inspire development in the field, making automated floor cleaning a reality for many households.

Chapter 8: DeepMind

A Chapter 8 on DeepMind would likely delve into this fascinating artificial intelligence research laboratory. Here's what you might find in such a chapter:

1. Introduction to DeepMind:

Founding and ownership: Established in the UK in 2010, acquired by Google in 2014, and merged with Google AI's Google Brain division in 2023 to form the current DeepMind.

Focus on Deep Learning: DeepMind is known for its pioneering work in Deep Learning, a subfield of Machine Learning using artificial neural networks inspired by the structure of the brain.

2. DeepMind's Achievements:

Breakthroughs in Games: AlphaGo, a DeepMind program, defeated the world champion Go player Lee Sedol in 2016, showcasing Deep Learning's potential in complex strategic games. Further advancements led to programs like AlphaStar mastering StarCraft II.

Protein Folding: DeepMind's AlphaFold program achieved a breakthrough in predicting protein structures, a critical challenge in biology and drug discovery.

Other Applications: DeepMind is involved in various applications, including healthcare (e.g., analyzing medical imagery), robotics, and energy modeling.

3. DeepMind's Technology:

Focus on Reinforcement Learning: DeepMind is a leader in developing and applying Reinforcement Learning, where an AI agent learns through trial and error to achieve goals in a simulated environment.

Advanced Neural Network Architectures: DeepMind researchers develop and utilize novel neural network architectures (e.g., transformers) to improve model performance on complex tasks.

Focus on Artificial General Intelligence (AGI): DeepMind has long-term aspirations of achieving AGI, which refers to an AI with human-level intelligence and adaptability.

4. DeepMind and Societal Impact:

Ethical Considerations: DeepMind's work raises ethical questions about AI safety, bias, and potential job displacement. The company emphasizes responsible AI development.

Open Collaboration: DeepMind balances open-source research with proprietary developments, fostering collaboration in the AI research community.

5. The Future of DeepMind:

Continued Research: DeepMind is likely to keep pushing boundaries in Deep Learning, Reinforcement Learning, and potentially AGI research.

Real-World Applications: Expect DeepMind's technology to be integrated into various real-world applications, impacting healthcare, robotics, and scientific discovery.

Further Exploration:

DeepMind Website: The DeepMind website offers news, research publications, and information about their work https://deepmind.google/.

DeepMind YouTube Channel: DeepMind's YouTube channel features videos explaining their research and applications https://www.youtube.com/@google_deepmind.

By exploring these topics, Chapter 8 on DeepMind would provide you with insights into this influential research lab and its contributions to the field of artificial intelligence.

8.1 AlphaGo defeats world champion Lee Sedol (2015)

Here's a breakdown of this milestone achievement:

Event: In March 2016, DeepMind's AlphaGo program emerged victorious in a five-game match against Lee Sedol, a world champion Go player.

Significance: This win marked a significant milestone in artificial intelligence (AI). Go is a complex strategy game with a vast number of possible moves, previously considered unmanageable for AI algorithms.

Impact: AlphaGo's success demonstrated the power of Deep Learning for complex strategic tasks and spurred further research in AI for games and other challenging domains.

While AlphaGo's development began around 2014, the historic match with Lee Sedol took place in 2016.

8.2 AlphaZero defeats the world's best chess and shogi engines (2017)

AlphaZero's Versatility: In late 2017, DeepMind introduced AlphaZero, a single AI system that could master multiple complex games with minimal human intervention.

Chess and Shogi Domination: AlphaZero trained from scratch using only the rules of the game and reinforcement learning through self-play. It then proceeded to defeat the world's strongest chess engine, Stockfish, and the best Shogi program, Elmo.

Unconventional Strategies: AlphaZero's victories were notable for its unconventional playing styles, showcasing the program's ability to learn and adapt beyond established strategies.

This achievement further solidified DeepMind's position at the forefront of AI research and highlighted the potential for generalizable AI systems capable of mastering diverse challenges.

You are correct! There's a slight modification to detail, but overall you've got it right. Here's a breakdown of DeepMind's achievement in protein folding:

AlphaFold's Impact: In 2021, DeepMind's AlphaFold 2 (technically an updated version of the original AlphaFold) significantly advanced the field of protein structure prediction, a longstanding challenge in biology.

Protein Folding Problem: Proteins are essential building blocks of life, and their function is heavily influenced by their 3D structure. Determining this structure through traditional methods can be slow and expensive. AlphaFold 2 achieved near atomic accuracy in predicting protein structures from just their amino acid sequence, a major breakthrough.

Benefits for Science and Medicine: This accomplishment has the potential to revolutionize various fields, including drug discovery, understanding diseases, and designing new materials. By efficiently predicting protein structures, scientists can gain deeper insights into their functions and develop new treatments or technologies.

It's important to note that AlphaFold refers to the general project, with AlphaFold 2 being a specific iteration that achieved this remarkable feat in 2021. DeepMind continues to develop and improve AlphaFold.

Chapter 9: The Impact of Artificial Intelligence

Artificial intelligence (AI) is rapidly transforming our world, impacting various aspects of society, industry, and even our daily lives. This chapter might explore these impacts in detail:

1. Positive Impacts of AI:

Efficiency and Automation: AI can automate repetitive tasks across industries, improving efficiency and productivity.

Enhanced Decision Making: AI can analyze vast amounts of data to identify patterns and trends, aiding in better decision-making in various fields (e.g., finance, healthcare).

Scientific Advancement: AI can assist in scientific research, enabling faster drug discovery, materials science exploration, and complex simulations.

Improved Quality of Life: AI applications like smart assistants, recommendation systems, and personalized learning can enhance our daily lives in various ways.

Robotic Assistance: Robots powered by AI can perform dangerous tasks, assist in surgery, and provide companionship for the elderly.

2. Challenges and Concerns:

Job Displacement: Automation through AI might lead to job displacement in certain sectors, requiring workforce retraining and adaptation.

Bias and Fairness: AI algorithms can perpetuate biases present in the data they are trained on, leading to discriminatory outcomes.

Explainability and Transparency: Understanding how complex AI models arrive at decisions can be challenging, raising concerns about accountability and fairness.

Privacy and Security: The increasing use of AI raises concerns about data privacy and security risks associated with collecting and storing vast amounts of personal information.

Existential Risks: Some experts express concerns about the potential for highly advanced AI to pose existential risks if not developed and deployed responsibly.

3. The Future of AI:

Responsible AI Development: Emphasis on ethical considerations, fairness, and transparency in AI development is crucial.

Human-AI Collaboration: The future may involve humans and AI working together, leveraging each other's strengths for optimal results.

Regulation and Governance: Developing frameworks to govern the use of AI and mitigate potential risks will be essential.

Focus on Beneficial AI: Directing AI research towards applications that benefit humanity and address global challenges is a priority.

4. Societal Considerations:

Education and Training: Equipping future generations with the skills to adapt to an AI-powered world will be crucial.

Addressing Inequality: AI advancements should be used to bridge societal divides and create a more equitable future.

Open Discussions: Encouraging public dialogue about the potential benefits and risks of AI is important for shaping its development and deployment.

By exploring these aspects, Chapter 9 would provide a comprehensive understanding of the multifaceted impact of AI on our world. It would encourage critical thinking about how we can harness the power of AI for a positive and prosperous future.

9.1 Expert Systems (1980s)

The Rise of Expert Systems:

The 1980s witnessed a surge in expert systems, a type of AI program designed to capture and replicate the knowledge and decision-making abilities of human experts in specific domains.

These systems relied on a knowledge base containing rules and facts, along with an inference engine to reason through the knowledge base and provide solutions to problems.

Applications of Expert Systems:

Expert systems found applications in various fields:

Medical Diagnosis: Systems aided doctors in diagnosing diseases by analyzing symptoms and medical history.

Financial Analysis: These systems helped assess financial risks and make investment recommendations.

Equipment Troubleshooting: Expert systems assisted technicians in diagnosing and repairing complex equipment.

Impact and Limitations:

Expert systems offered benefits like improved decision-making, consistency, and faster problem-solving in specific domains.

However, limitations emerged:

Knowledge Acquisition Bottleneck: Capturing and encoding expert knowledge into the system was a time-consuming and expensive process.

Limited Domain Expertise: Expert systems excelled in specific areas but struggled with broader or unforeseen situations.

Maintenance Challenges: Keeping the knowledge base up-to-date with advancements in the field proved challenging.

Legacy of Expert Systems:

Despite their limitations, expert systems laid the groundwork for knowledge-based AI and paved the way for more sophisticated reasoning systems.

They demonstrated the potential for AI to assist humans in complex problem-solving tasks within defined domains.

Connecting to the Bigger Picture:

This section on expert systems in the 1980s could connect to the broader chapter theme of AI's impact by highlighting:

The early promise of AI in replicating human expertise.

The challenges of knowledge representation and reasoning.

The importance of considering limitations alongside potential benefits when developing and deploying AI technologies.

Further Exploration:

Expert System (Wikipedia): https://en.wikipedia.org/wiki/Expert_system provides a more detailed overview of expert systems.

A brief history and technical review of the expert system research:

https://iopscience.iop.org/article/10.1088/1757-899X/242/1/012111 explores the historical development and technical aspects of expert systems.

9.2 IBM's Deep Blue defeats chess world champion Kasparov (1997)

That's right! An important event in the history of AI and Chapter 9: The Impact of Artificial Intelligence would likely cover IBM's Deep Blue defeating chess world champion Garry Kasparov in 1997. Here's a breakdown of its significance:

A Milestone in AI Achievement:

Deep Blue, a chess-playing computer developed by IBM, defeated Garry Kasparov, the reigning world champion, in a six-game match in 1997. This victory was a significant milestone in artificial intelligence.

Prioritizing Brute Force: Deep Blue's success relied on brute force computing power, analyzing millions of chess positions per second. It didn't necessarily represent human-like strategic thinking but showcased the potential of AI to surpass human capabilities in specific domains.

Impact and Controversy:

Public Fascination: This event sparked public fascination with the capabilities of AI and its potential to compete with humans in intellectual tasks.

Debate about "True" Intelligence: While impressive, Deep Blue's victory reignited debates about the definition of intelligence. Did it truly understand chess, or was it simply a powerful pattern-matching machine?

Future Directions for AI: Deep Blue's win motivated further research into AI, but it also highlighted the need to explore AI beyond brute force computation and move towards more human-like reasoning and problem-solving.

Connecting to the Bigger Picture:

This section on Deep Blue's victory could connect to the broader chapter theme of AI's impact by:

Demonstrating the increasing capabilities of AI in specific tasks.

Raising questions about the nature of intelligence and the benchmarks for measuring AI progress.

Highlighting the ongoing debate about the potential benefits and challenges of advanced AI.

Further Exploration:

Deep Blue versus Garry Kasparov (Wikipedia): https://en.wikipedia.org/wiki/Deep_Blue_versus_Garry_Kasparov provides a detailed account of the match and its historical context.

Deep Blue | IBM: https://www.ibm.com/history/deep-blue offers information about Deep Blue's development and technical details from IBM's perspective.

9.3 IBM's Watson defeats two former Jeopardy! champions (2011)

Watson's Challenge:

In 2 televised matches in February 2011, IBM's Watson, a question-answering computer system, competed against Ken Jennings and Brad Rutter, the two most successful Jeopardy! champions at the time.

Unlike Deep Blue, Watson wasn't a brute-force machine. It relied on natural language processing, information retrieval, and deep learning to understand clues and generate responses.

A Victory for Language Understanding:

Watson's triumph showcased significant progress in AI's ability to understand and respond to natural language. It could process complex clues, identify relevant information, and generate phrased responses in a way that was competitive with human champions.

Impact and Implications:

This event highlighted the potential of AI for tasks beyond games. Watson's technology could be applied in areas like information retrieval, customer service chatbots, and education.

However, limitations remained. Watson struggled with some types of clues requiring cultural understanding or common sense reasoning.

Connecting to the Bigger Picture:

This section on Watson's Jeopardy! win could connect to the broader theme of AI's impact by:

Demonstrating advancements in AI's ability to understand and respond to natural language.

Highlighting the potential applications of AI in various domains beyond games and entertainment.

Underscoring the ongoing need for AI development to address limitations like common-sense reasoning and adaptability.

Further Exploration:

Watson, Jeopardy! champion | IBM: https://www.ibm.com/history/watson-jeopardy provides information about Watson's development and its performance on Jeopardy! from IBM's perspective.

IBM Watson (Wikipedia): https://en.wikipedia.org/wiki/IBM_Watson offers a more general overview of Watson's technology and applications.

Chapter 10: The Future of Artificial Intelligence

As artificial intelligence (AI) continues to evolve rapidly, Chapter 10 would likely explore the exciting possibilities and potential challenges that lie ahead. Here's a glimpse into what such a chapter might cover:

1. Potential Applications of Advanced AI:

Enhanced Healthcare: AI could revolutionize healthcare through earlier disease detection, personalized medicine, and robotic surgery assistance.

Smarter Cities: AI-powered traffic management, optimized resource allocation, and improved public safety could lead to more efficient and livable cities.

Scientific Discovery: AI can analyze vast datasets and generate hypotheses, accelerating scientific progress in various fields.

Personalized Learning: AI-powered tutoring systems could adapt to individual student needs, enhancing the learning experience.

Environmental Sustainability: AI can help optimize energy use, monitor environmental changes, and develop sustainable solutions.

2. Emerging Trends in AI Research:

Explainable AI (XAI): Developing AI models that are more transparent and understandable to humans, crucial for building trust and ensuring responsible use.

Artificial General Intelligence (AGI): The quest to create AI with human-level intelligence and adaptability across various domains.

Human-AI Collaboration: Exploring how humans and AI can work together to achieve optimal results, leveraging each other's strengths.

Neuromorphic Computing: Developing hardware inspired by the human brain, potentially leading to more efficient and powerful AI systems.

AI Safety and Security: Addressing potential risks associated with advanced AI, such as bias, misuse, and unintended consequences.

3. Ethical Considerations:

Job displacement by automation: Strategies for retraining and upskilling the workforce to adapt to a changing job market.

Algorithmic bias and fairness: Ensuring AI algorithms are developed and deployed in a way that is fair and unbiased.

Privacy concerns: Balancing the benefits of AI with the need to protect individual privacy and data security.

The control and ownership of AI: Establishing frameworks for responsible development, ownership, and deployment of powerful AI systems.

4. The Long-Term Future of AI:

Impact on Society: AI has the potential to reshape societies in profound ways. This section might explore potential scenarios and the importance of shaping AI development towards beneficial outcomes for humanity.

Singularity and Existential Risks: Some experts express concerns about a potential "singularity" where AI surpasses human intelligence and poses existential risks. This section might explore these views and emphasize the importance of responsible AI development to mitigate risks.

5. Conclusion:

The concluding section might emphasize the need for a collaborative approach to AI development. This would involve researchers, policymakers, industry leaders, and the public working together to ensure AI benefits all of humanity.

Further Exploration:

Future of Life Institute: https://futureoflife.org explores existential risks from advanced technologies, including AI.

Partnership on AI: https://partnershiponai.org is a global effort to ensure the beneficial development and use of AI.

This chapter would provide a thought-provoking exploration of the potential future of AI, encouraging readers to consider its vast possibilities and the importance of responsible development for a brighter future.

10.1 OpenAI releases GPT-3 (2020)

OpenAI's GPT-3: A Powerful Language Model

Released in 2020, OpenAI's GPT-3 (Generative Pre-trained Transformer 3) is a powerful large language model known for its ability to generate realistic and coherent text.

Advancements in NLP: GPT-3, with its 175 billion parameters (a measure of model complexity), represented a significant step forward in Natural Language Processing (NLP). It could perform a wide range of tasks like

text generation

translation

writing different kinds of creative content

answering your questions in an informative way (like I am doing now!)

Impact and Implications:

GPT-3's capabilities sparked excitement about the potential applications of advanced language models. It showcased the potential for AI to:

Revolutionize human-computer interaction

Personalize education and learning

Enhance creative writing and content generation

However, concerns emerged regarding potential misuse, such as generating fake news or biased content.

Connecting to the Future of AI:

The inclusion of GPT-3 in this chapter could connect to the broader discussion of the future of AI in a few ways:

Highlighting advancements in AI capabilities: GPT-3 exemplifies the rapid progress being made in AI, particularly in language processing.

Exploring the potential benefits of AI for communication and creativity: Language models like GPT-3 have the potential to transform how we interact with information and create content.

Underscoring the importance of responsible AI development: The potential for misuse of GPT-3 emphasizes the need for careful consideration of ethical implications as AI continues to evolve.

By including GPT-3, this chapter would provide a more comprehensive picture of the exciting possibilities and challenges that lie ahead in the realm of AI, specifically in language processing.

10.2 Google's LaMDA (2023)

LaMDA: Google's Conversational AI Model (2023)

In 2023, Google introduced LaMDA, a factual language model focused on dialogue applications. It aims to generate natural and engaging conversation by being informative and comprehensive.

Focus on Dialogue: LaMDA is specifically trained for dialogue tasks, allowing it to hold informative conversations on various topics. It can access and process information from Google Search to provide comprehensive responses.

LaMDA and the Future of AI:

LaMDA's conversational capabilities contribute to the development of more natural and engaging human-computer interaction. This could lead to advancements in:

Chatbots and virtual assistants

Educational tools and personalized learning platforms

Customer service applications

LaMDA's development also raises questions about the potential for bias in AI models and the importance of ensuring factual accuracy in information retrieval.

Connecting to Other Advancements:

The inclusion of LaMDA can connect to other aspects of the chapter on the future of AI:

Reinforcing the trend of AI for communication: LaMDA, alongside GPT-3 and other language models, exemplifies the growing focus on AI for communication and natural language processing.

Highlighting the importance of Explainable AI (XAI): As AI models become more complex, ensuring users understand how LaMDA arrives at its responses becomes crucial for building trust and transparency.

By discussing LaMDA, this chapter would provide a well-rounded perspective on the future of AI, specifically regarding the potential for more natural and informative human-computer interaction through advanced dialogue models.

10.3 Legal issues around AI art creation (2023)

The Rise of AI Art and Legal Uncertainties (2023)

The growing popularity of AI-generated art raises a multitude of legal questions that are yet to be fully addressed. Here are some key areas of concern:

Copyright Ownership: Who owns the copyright to art created by AI? Is it the programmer, the user who prompts the AI, or the AI itself? Current copyright law in many countries focuses on human authorship, making it unclear how AI art fits in.

Artistic Merit: Can AI-generated art be considered truly creative or original, or is it simply a derivative work based on the data it's trained on? This question has implications for copyright protection.

Moral Rights: Do AI artists have moral rights to their creations, similar to the rights granted to human artists? This includes rights like attribution and the right to prevent modification of their work.

Liability: Who is liable if AI art infringes on existing copyrights? Is it the user, the developer of the AI program, or both?

Recent Developments (2023): In 2023, the US Copyright Office issued guidance reiterating the human authorship requirement for copyright protection. However, it acknowledges that human curation and selection of AI-generated content might be enough to establish authorship in certain cases.

The Road Ahead:

The legal landscape surrounding AI art is still under development. This section could discuss potential future scenarios:

Evolving Copyright Law: Copyright laws might need to be revised to address the specificities of AI-generated art.

Focus on Transparency: Clear guidelines and disclosures around the use of AI in art creation might be necessary.

Importance of Human Collaboration: The chapter could emphasize that AI art is most impactful when it fosters human creativity and collaboration.

Further Exploration:

Article: Ask the Expert: What are legal issues surrounding AI, its impact on the arts?:
https://news.iu.edu/live/news/31788-the-art-in-artificial-intelligence-

eskenazi-school-cou provides insights from an Intellectual Property Law professor.

The Legal Implications of AI Generated Artwork: https://larc.cardozo.yu.edu/cgi/viewcontent.cgi?article=1346&context=aelj-blog offers a legal analysis of AI art and copyright issues.

By including this section, Chapter 10 would acknowledge the fascinating world of AI art creation while also highlighting the legal uncertainties that need to be addressed as this technology continues to evolve.

Conclusion

Recap and Looking Forward:

This chapter has explored the vast potential of artificial intelligence, from its potential to revolutionize various fields to the exciting possibilities for human-computer collaboration. We've also discussed the challenges and ethical considerations that need to be addressed as AI continues to evolve.

The Importance of Responsible Development:

As we move forward, it's crucial to ensure that AI development is done responsibly, with a focus on transparency, fairness, and alignment with human values. Collaboration between researchers, policymakers, industry leaders, and the public is essential to ensure that AI benefits all of humanity.

A Call to Action:

The future of AI is not predetermined. We have the opportunity to shape its development and ensure it serves as a tool for progress and positive change. By fostering open discussions, considering the ethical implications, and prioritizing responsible development, we can ensure that AI becomes a force for good in the years to come.

Optional Additions:

Briefly mention some ongoing research initiatives focused on responsible AI development.

End with a thought-provoking question to encourage readers to consider their own hopes and concerns about the future of AI.

By concluding on a hopeful note while emphasizing the importance of responsible development, this chapter would leave readers with a sense of agency and inspire them to engage in further exploration of this rapidly evolving field.

www.ingramcontent.com/pod-product-compliance
Lightning Source LLC
Chambersburg PA
CBHW072053230526
45479CB00010B/924